PASSIVE INCOME POWERHOUSE

Real Estate Riches on Autopilot

NELLA BYRAN

Copyright

No part of this should be reproduced without the permission of the author.

© Nella Byran 2024

Contents

Introduction 4
Chapter 1: The Power of Passive Income in Real Estate 7
Chapter 2: Unlocking the Potential 10
Chapter 3: The Blueprint for Real Estate Riches on Autopilot .. 13
Chapter 4: Leveraging Automation 17
Chapter 5: Finding Your Passive Income Powerhouse 21
Chapter 6: The Art of Passive Real Estate Investing Mastery ... 25
Chapter 7: Maximizing Returns with Minimal Effort 29
Chapter 8: Crafting Your Passive Income Portfolio................... 33
Chapter 9: Tax Optimization Tactics for Passive Wealth Preservation 37
Chapter 10: Navigating Market Trends for Maximum Passive Income Growth 41
Chapter 11: Maverick Negotiation Tactics for Passive Real Estate Success 45
Chapter 12: Tools for Passive Income Powerhouses 49
Chapter 13: Overcoming Passive Income Challenges................ 53
Chapter 14: The Passive Income Powerhouse's Guide to Property Management 57
Chapter 15: Scaling Your Passive Income Empire 62
Chapter 16: Your Journey to Real Estate Riches on Autopilot .. 67
Conclusion 73

Introduction

Welcome to "Passive Income Powerhouse: Real Estate Riches on Autopilot," where we embark on a transformative journey into the realm of real estate investment, exploring the art and science of generating wealth through passive income streams. In these pages, you'll discover the blueprint for building an empire of financial independence, leveraging the timeless power of real estate to create sustainable wealth without the need for constant manual effort.

Real estate has long been revered as a cornerstone of wealth creation, offering unparalleled opportunities for those who understand its dynamics. At the heart of this book lies the recognition of passive income's transformative potential, where money works for you, rather than the other way around. Whether you're a seasoned investor seeking to optimize your portfolio or a newcomer eager to unlock the secrets of passive wealth accumulation, this book serves as your comprehensive guide to success in the dynamic world of real estate.

The journey begins by delving into the foundational principles of passive income in real estate, illuminating its unparalleled potential to provide financial freedom and security. From there, we delve into the strategies and tactics necessary to unlock this potential, from identifying profitable properties to mastering the art of negotiation and leveraging automation for maximum efficiency.

With a keen focus on practicality and real-world application, each chapter equips you with the knowledge and tools needed to navigate the complexities of passive real estate investing with confidence and finesse. From crafting a diversified portfolio to optimizing tax strategies and overcoming common challenges, you'll learn how to harness the full power of passive income to achieve your financial goals.

But this book is more than just a manual for wealth creation—it's a roadmap for personal and professional growth. As you journey through its pages, you'll not only gain invaluable insights into the mechanics of passive income generation but also cultivate the mindset and resilience necessary to thrive in any market environment.

Whether you're a seasoned investor looking to take your portfolio to new heights or a newcomer eager to embark on your first real estate venture, "Passive Income Powerhouse" is your indispensable companion on the path to financial independence. So, join us as we embark on a journey to real estate riches on autopilot, where the possibilities are as endless as your ambition.

Chapter 1: The Power of Passive Income in Real Estate

In the opening chapter of "Passive Income Powerhouse: Real Estate Riches on Autopilot," we delve deep into the transformative potential of passive income within the realm of real estate investment. Here, we lay the foundation for understanding why passive income is not just a financial concept but a life-changing strategy that can redefine your relationship with wealth and work.

Passive income, often hailed as the holy grail of financial freedom, holds a unique allure in the world of real estate. Unlike active income, which requires ongoing time and effort to earn, passive income allows you to generate wealth with minimal ongoing involvement. This distinction is particularly pronounced in real estate, where the right investments can yield consistent cash flow streams that require little to no daily management.

At the heart of the power of passive income lies the concept of leverage. Real estate offers unparalleled opportunities to multiply your wealth through the strategic use of borrowed capital. By utilizing leverage responsibly, investors can amplify their returns and accelerate the growth of their passive income streams, effectively multiplying the impact of their initial investment.

Furthermore, passive income in real estate provides a hedge against inflation and market volatility. Unlike traditional investments like stocks or bonds, which may fluctuate in value based on external market forces, real estate assets have the potential to appreciate over time, providing a reliable source of long-term wealth accumulation.

But perhaps the most compelling aspect of passive income in real estate is its ability to afford investors the gift of time freedom. By building a portfolio of income-generating properties, individuals can gradually liberate themselves from the constraints of traditional employment, reclaiming their time to pursue passions, spend with loved ones, or simply enjoy life on their own terms.

In this chapter, we explore real-world examples of individuals who have unlocked the power of passive income in real estate to achieve financial independence and beyond. Through their stories, we gain valuable insights into the mindset and strategies necessary to harness this transformative force for ourselves.

Ultimately, "The Power of Passive Income in Real Estate" sets the stage for the journey ahead, inviting readers to reimagine their relationship with wealth and work as they embark on a quest for real estate riches on autopilot. So, join us as we explore the boundless possibilities that await those who dare to embrace the power of passive income in the world of real estate.

Chapter 2: Unlocking the Potential

In the second chapter of "Passive Income Powerhouse: Real Estate Riches on Autopilot," we delve into the actionable steps and strategies necessary to unlock the full potential of passive income and lay the foundation for building your own empire of wealth through real estate.

Building a passive income empire requires a combination of vision, strategy, and execution. It begins with a clear understanding of your financial goals and objectives, as well as a realistic assessment of your current resources and constraints. By defining your investment criteria and risk tolerance, you can develop a roadmap that aligns with your long-term aspirations.

Central to unlocking the potential of passive income in real estate is the concept of scalability. Unlike traditional forms of employment, where your earning potential may be limited by factors such as time or market demand, real estate offers virtually limitless opportunities for growth and expansion. By adopting a scalable approach to investing, you can gradually increase the size and scope of your portfolio, compounding your wealth over time.

Another key aspect of building your passive income empire is diversification. While real estate can be a lucrative investment vehicle, it's important to avoid putting all your eggs in one basket. By diversifying your portfolio across different asset classes, locations, and investment strategies, you can mitigate risk and maximize returns, ensuring long-term sustainability and stability.

Furthermore, successful real estate investing requires a keen understanding of market dynamics and trends. By staying abreast of economic indicators, demographic shifts, and regulatory changes, you can position yourself to capitalize on emerging opportunities and navigate potential challenges with confidence and agility.

But perhaps the most important ingredient in building your passive income empire is action. While planning and preparation are essential, they mean little without the willingness to take decisive steps towards your goals. Whether it's conducting due diligence on potential investment properties, negotiating favorable terms, or implementing innovative strategies to optimize cash flow, success in real estate requires a proactive and resourceful mindset.

In this chapter, we provide practical guidance and real-world examples to help you unlock the potential of passive income and embark on your journey towards building a sustainable and thriving empire of wealth through real estate. So, join us as we explore the strategies and tactics necessary to turn your dreams of financial independence into reality, one property at a time.

Chapter 3: The Blueprint for Real Estate Riches on Autopilot

In the third chapter of "Passive Income Powerhouse: Real Estate Riches on Autopilot," we unveil the blueprint for achieving real estate wealth with minimal hands-on involvement, paving the way for a truly passive income stream.

Crafting a blueprint for real estate riches begins with setting clear, achievable goals. Whether your aim is to achieve financial independence, retire early, or simply build a legacy for future generations, having a well-defined roadmap is essential for success. By outlining specific objectives and milestones, you can chart a course that aligns with your vision and values.

Central to the blueprint for real estate riches is the concept of leverage. By intelligently utilizing other people's money (OPM), such as mortgage financing, investors can amplify their purchasing power and maximize returns on their initial investment. This allows for the acquisition of multiple properties with minimal out-of-pocket expenses, accelerating the growth of your real estate portfolio.

Moreover, the blueprint emphasizes the importance of passive income streams that require little to no ongoing management. This may involve investing in rental properties, where tenants provide a steady stream of cash flow, or leveraging technology and automation to streamline property management tasks. By focusing on assets that generate consistent and reliable income without the need for constant supervision, investors can free up their time and energy to pursue other interests or ventures.

Another key component of the blueprint for real estate riches is risk management. While real estate can offer attractive returns, it's not without its challenges and uncertainties. From market fluctuations to unexpected maintenance issues, there are numerous factors that can impact the performance of your investments. By diversifying your portfolio, maintaining adequate reserves, and implementing sound risk mitigation strategies, you can safeguard your wealth and protect against potential downturns.

Furthermore, the blueprint emphasizes the importance of continuous learning and adaptation. The real estate landscape is constantly evolving, with new trends, technologies, and regulations shaping the way investors operate. By staying informed and open to innovation, you can position yourself to capitalize on emerging opportunities and stay ahead of the curve.

In this chapter, we provide a step-by-step guide to creating your own blueprint for real estate riches on autopilot. From setting goals and leveraging other people's money to managing risk and embracing innovation, we cover all the essential elements necessary to build a sustainable and thriving real estate empire. So, join us as we unlock the secrets to achieving financial freedom through passive income in the dynamic world of real estate.

Chapter 4: Leveraging Automation

In the fourth chapter of "Passive Income Powerhouse: Real Estate Riches on Autopilot," we explore the pivotal role of automation in achieving passive wealth accumulation within the realm of real estate investment. This chapter delves into innovative strategies and cutting-edge technologies that enable investors to streamline their operations, optimize efficiency, and maximize returns with minimal manual intervention.

Automation has emerged as a game-changer in the world of real estate, offering unprecedented opportunities for investors to scale their operations and generate passive income streams with ease. From property management software to artificial intelligence-driven analytics, today's investors have access to a wealth of tools and technologies that empower them to work smarter, not harder.

One of the primary areas where automation revolutionizes real estate investment is in property management. Traditionally, managing rental properties required significant time and effort, from screening tenants and collecting rent to scheduling maintenance and repairs. However, with the advent of property management software and online platforms, many of these tasks can now be automated, allowing investors to oversee their portfolios remotely and with minimal hands-on involvement.

Moreover, automation extends beyond just property management to encompass various aspects of the investment process. For instance, investors can leverage algorithms and predictive analytics to identify lucrative investment opportunities and assess risk factors more accurately. This data-driven approach not only saves time but also enhances decision-making, enabling investors to make more informed choices and optimize their returns.

Furthermore, automation enables investors to implement sophisticated strategies for passive wealth accumulation, such as cash-out refinancing and 1031 exchanges, with greater efficiency and precision. By automating the documentation and transactional processes involved in these strategies, investors can capitalize on market opportunities and optimize their capital deployment strategies without being bogged down by administrative burdens.

However, while automation offers immense potential for passive wealth accumulation, it's essential to approach it with a strategic mindset and a keen awareness of its limitations. Not all tasks can or should be automated, and human oversight remains crucial for ensuring compliance, managing relationships, and adapting to changing market conditions.

In this chapter, we provide practical guidance and real-world examples to help investors leverage automation effectively in their quest for passive wealth accumulation through real estate. From selecting the right tools and technologies to implementing best practices and mitigating risks, we cover all the essential strategies necessary to harness the full power of automation in the pursuit of financial independence. So, join us as we explore the transformative potential of automation in building your passive income empire in the dynamic world of real estate.

Chapter 5: Finding Your Passive Income Powerhouse

In the fifth chapter of "Passive Income Powerhouse: Real Estate Riches on Autopilot," we embark on a journey to uncover the fundamental strategies and techniques for identifying profitable properties, essential for building a sustainable and thriving passive income portfolio.

The cornerstone of successful real estate investing lies in the ability to identify properties that possess the potential to generate consistent and reliable passive income streams. However, with countless options available in the market, finding the right investment opportunities can be a daunting task. This chapter aims to demystify the process and provide investors with the tools and insights needed to navigate the complexities of property selection with confidence and clarity.

At the heart of identifying profitable properties is a thorough understanding of market dynamics and trends. By conducting comprehensive market research and analysis, investors can identify areas with strong demand for rental properties and favorable supply-demand dynamics. Factors such as population growth, job opportunities, and infrastructure development can all influence the long-term appreciation potential and rental income of a property.

Moreover, investors must consider the financial metrics and performance indicators that determine the profitability of a potential investment. These include metrics such as cash-on-cash return, cap rate, and gross rent multiplier, which provide valuable insights into the expected return on investment and cash flow potential of a property. By conducting a detailed financial analysis, investors can assess the viability of a property and make informed decisions based on its income-generating potential.

In addition to financial considerations, investors must also evaluate the physical characteristics and condition of a property. Factors such as location, property type, and amenities can all impact its appeal to tenants and its ability to command competitive rental rates. Furthermore, investors should assess the property's maintenance and repair needs, as well as any potential regulatory or compliance issues that may affect its long-term profitability.

Furthermore, investors can leverage technology and data-driven insights to streamline the property selection process and identify hidden gems in the market. From online listing platforms to real estate analytics tools, today's investors have access to a wealth of resources that can facilitate their search for profitable properties and enhance their decision-making process.

In this chapter, we provide practical guidance and real-world examples to help investors navigate the process of identifying profitable properties and building a diversified portfolio of income-generating assets. By mastering the art of property selection, investors can lay the foundation for long-term success and unlock the full potential of passive income in the dynamic world of real estate. So, join us as we embark on a journey to find your passive income powerhouse and achieve financial independence through strategic property investments.

Chapter 6: The Art of Passive Real Estate Investing Mastery

In the sixth chapter of "Passive Income Powerhouse: Real Estate Riches on Autopilot," we delve into the nuanced techniques and mindset required to master the art of passive real estate investing. This chapter is dedicated to equipping investors with the knowledge and skills needed to navigate the intricacies of the real estate market with finesse and confidence, ultimately unlocking the full potential of passive income generation.

Passive real estate investing is as much an art as it is a science. While it involves leveraging data and analysis to make informed decisions, it also requires intuition, creativity, and a deep understanding of human behavior. Mastery in this field entails developing a holistic approach that combines analytical rigor with emotional intelligence, allowing investors to navigate the complexities of real estate investing with clarity and poise.

At the core of passive real estate investing mastery lies the ability to cultivate a long-term mindset and stay focused on the bigger picture. While short-term fluctuations and market volatility are inevitable, successful investors maintain a steadfast commitment to their goals and objectives, weathering the ups and downs of the market with resilience and determination.

Moreover, mastery in passive real estate investing involves the art of effective risk management. While real estate can offer attractive returns, it's not without its risks and uncertainties. Successful investors understand the importance of diversification, asset allocation, and risk mitigation strategies in safeguarding their wealth and preserving their capital in the face of potential challenges.

Furthermore, mastery in passive real estate investing requires a commitment to continuous learning and growth. The real estate market is constantly evolving, with new trends, technologies, and regulations shaping the way investors operate. By staying informed and open to innovation, investors can adapt to changing market conditions and capitalize on emerging opportunities with agility and foresight.

In addition to technical skills, mastery in passive real estate investing also involves the art of effective communication and relationship building. From negotiating favorable deals to managing tenant relationships, successful investors understand the importance of building trust and rapport with stakeholders, fostering mutually beneficial partnerships that contribute to long-term success.

In this chapter, we provide practical guidance and real-world examples to help investors master the art of passive real estate investing. From developing a strategic mindset to honing negotiation skills and cultivating resilience, we cover all the essential elements necessary to achieve mastery in the dynamic and rewarding world of real estate. So, join us as we explore the art of passive real estate investing mastery and unlock the keys to financial independence and wealth accumulation.

Chapter 7: Maximizing Returns with Minimal Effort

In the seventh chapter of "Passive Income Powerhouse: Real Estate Riches on Autopilot," we delve into the strategies and principles that enable passive investors to optimize returns while minimizing their involvement in day-to-day operations. This chapter serves as a comprehensive guide for those seeking to build wealth through real estate without sacrificing their time or energy.

Passive investing in real estate offers a compelling proposition: the opportunity to generate significant returns with minimal effort. However, achieving this requires a strategic approach that prioritizes efficiency, automation, and delegation. The Passive Investor's Guide distills the essential principles and techniques necessary to maximize returns while maintaining a hands-off approach to management.

One of the key strategies explored in this guide is the principle of leverage. By leveraging other people's time, expertise, and resources, passive investors can amplify their returns and scale their investment portfolios without being bogged down by the day-to-day responsibilities of property management. This may involve partnering with professional property management companies or investing in real estate syndications and funds that pool capital from multiple investors.

Moreover, the Passive Investor's Guide emphasizes the importance of passive income streams that require minimal ongoing management. This may involve investing in turnkey properties or real estate investment trusts (REITs), which offer exposure to diversified portfolios of income-generating properties without the need for hands-on involvement in property management or tenant relations.

Furthermore, the guide explores the concept of passive real estate investing through crowdfunding platforms, which enable investors to participate in real estate projects with relatively low minimum investment thresholds and minimal administrative burden. By leveraging technology and online platforms, passive investors can access a diverse range of investment opportunities and build a well-rounded portfolio with ease.

Additionally, the Passive Investor's Guide highlights the importance of due diligence and risk management in passive real estate investing. While passive investing offers the allure of minimal effort, it's essential for investors to conduct thorough research and analysis to assess the viability and risk profile of potential investments. By carefully vetting opportunities and diversifying their portfolios, passive investors can mitigate risk and safeguard their wealth over the long term.

In this chapter, we provide practical advice, tips, and best practices to help passive investors maximize returns while minimizing their involvement in real estate investment activities. From leveraging leverage to exploring passive income opportunities and managing risk effectively, the Passive Investor's Guide equips investors with the knowledge and tools needed to build wealth through real estate with minimal effort. So, join us as we explore the art of passive investing and unlock the keys to financial freedom and prosperity.

Chapter 8: Crafting Your Passive Income Portfolio

In the eighth chapter of "Passive Income Powerhouse: Real Estate Riches on Autopilot," we explore the critical role of diversification in building a resilient and sustainable passive income portfolio. This chapter is dedicated to guiding investors through the process of crafting a well-rounded portfolio that balances risk and return while maximizing opportunities for wealth accumulation.

Diversification is a fundamental principle of investing that involves spreading risk across different assets, industries, and geographic regions. In the context of real estate, diversification serves as a safeguard against market volatility and unexpected events that may impact individual properties or sectors. Crafting a diversified passive income portfolio is essential for protecting capital, minimizing downside risk, and maximizing long-term returns.

One of the key diversification strategies explored in this chapter is asset class diversification. Rather than focusing exclusively on one type of real estate investment, such as residential properties or commercial properties, investors can diversify their portfolios by allocating capital across different asset classes. This may include investing in multifamily residential properties, office buildings, retail centers, industrial warehouses, and other types of real estate assets, each with its own risk-return profile and income-generating potential.

Moreover, geographic diversification is another essential component of crafting a diversified passive income portfolio. By investing in properties located in different markets and regions, investors can mitigate the impact of localized economic downturns, regulatory changes, or other factors that may affect property values or rental demand. Geographic diversification allows investors to spread risk across a broader range of markets and capitalize on opportunities for growth in different regions.

Furthermore, diversification across investment strategies is essential for building a robust passive income portfolio. In addition to traditional buy-and-hold rental properties, investors may consider alternative strategies such as real estate crowdfunding, real estate investment trusts (REITs), and real estate syndications. Each of these investment vehicles offers unique advantages and opportunities for income generation, allowing investors to diversify their portfolios and optimize returns.

Additionally, diversification in terms of tenant demographics and property types can further enhance the resilience of a passive income portfolio. By investing in properties that cater to different tenant profiles, such as young professionals, families, or retirees, investors can reduce reliance on any single demographic group and minimize the impact of tenant turnover or economic fluctuations.

In this chapter, we provide practical guidance and real-world examples to help investors craft a diversified passive income portfolio that aligns with their financial goals and risk tolerance. From asset class diversification to geographic diversification and beyond, we explore the strategies and techniques necessary to build a resilient and sustainable portfolio that generates consistent income and long-term wealth. So, join us as we explore the art of diversification and unlock the keys to financial success in the dynamic world of real estate investing.

Chapter 9: Tax Optimization Tactics for Passive Wealth Preservation

In the ninth chapter of "Passive Income Powerhouse: Real Estate Riches on Autopilot," we delve into the intricate world of tax optimization tactics for preserving and maximizing passive wealth generated through real estate investments. This chapter aims to provide investors with the knowledge and strategies necessary to minimize tax liabilities, optimize returns, and enhance overall portfolio performance.

Real estate investing offers numerous tax advantages and incentives that can significantly impact an investor's bottom line. From deductions and depreciation allowances to tax-deferred exchanges and capital gains tax exemptions, understanding and leveraging these tax optimization tactics is essential for maximizing after-tax returns and preserving wealth over the long term.

One of the most powerful tax optimization tactics available to real estate investors is the ability to leverage depreciation deductions to offset rental income. Depreciation allows investors to deduct a portion of the cost of their property over time, reducing taxable income and lowering overall tax liabilities. By strategically maximizing depreciation allowances and leveraging cost segregation studies, investors can further enhance their tax efficiency and preserve more of their passive income for wealth accumulation.

Moreover, tax-deferred exchanges, such as the 1031 exchange, offer investors the opportunity to defer capital gains taxes when selling one investment property and reinvesting the proceeds into another like-kind property. By deferring taxes on property sales, investors can maximize their reinvestment potential and compound returns over time, effectively enhancing portfolio growth and wealth accumulation.

Additionally, real estate investors can leverage passive losses and credits to offset taxable income from other sources. Passive losses generated through rental properties can be used to offset passive income from other investments, such as dividends or capital gains, reducing overall tax liabilities and optimizing after-tax returns. Furthermore, tax credits, such as the low-income housing tax credit or energy-efficient tax credits, offer additional opportunities for tax optimization and wealth preservation.

Furthermore, tax optimization tactics extend beyond just income taxes to encompass estate planning and asset protection strategies. By structuring real estate investments effectively and leveraging estate planning tools such as trusts and LLCs, investors can minimize estate taxes, protect assets from creditors, and ensure a smooth transfer of wealth to future generations.

In this chapter, we provide practical guidance and real-world examples to help investors navigate the complex landscape of tax optimization tactics for passive wealth preservation. From maximizing depreciation deductions to leveraging tax-deferred exchanges and implementing effective estate planning strategies, we cover all the essential elements necessary to minimize tax liabilities and preserve wealth over the long term. So, join us as we explore the art of tax optimization and unlock the keys to financial success in the dynamic world of real estate investing.

Chapter 10: Navigating Market Trends for Maximum Passive Income Growth

In the tenth chapter of "Passive Income Powerhouse: Real Estate Riches on Autopilot," we embark on a journey to understand how market trends impact passive income growth in real estate investments. This chapter is dedicated to equipping investors with the knowledge and strategies necessary to navigate market dynamics effectively, capitalize on emerging opportunities, and maximize passive income growth.

Real estate markets are dynamic and constantly evolving, influenced by a myriad of factors including economic conditions, demographic trends, and regulatory changes. Successful investors understand the importance of staying informed and proactive in monitoring market trends, identifying potential opportunities, and adapting their investment strategies accordingly.

One of the key market trends that investors must navigate is the overall economic climate. Economic indicators such as GDP growth, employment rates, and inflation can have a significant impact on real estate markets, influencing demand for rental properties and rental rates. By staying abreast of economic trends and forecasts, investors can position themselves to capitalize on opportunities for passive income growth and mitigate risks associated with economic downturns.

Moreover, demographic trends play a crucial role in shaping real estate market dynamics. Shifts in population growth, migration patterns, and lifestyle preferences can drive demand for certain types of properties and locations, presenting opportunities for investors to capitalize on emerging trends. For example, the rise of remote work and urbanization trends may create demand for rental properties in suburban or secondary markets, while demographic shifts towards an aging population may increase demand for senior housing or assisted living facilities.

Furthermore, regulatory changes and policy developments can impact real estate markets and investment opportunities. Changes in zoning regulations, tax policies, or rent control laws can affect property values, rental rates, and overall investment returns. By staying informed about regulatory developments and understanding their potential implications, investors can adjust their investment strategies accordingly and mitigate risks associated with regulatory uncertainty.

In addition to monitoring external market trends, successful investors also understand the importance of conducting thorough market research and due diligence when evaluating potential investment opportunities. By analyzing market fundamentals such as supply and demand dynamics, vacancy rates, and rental trends, investors can identify markets and properties with strong income-generating potential and position themselves for maximum passive income growth.

In this chapter, we provide practical guidance and real-world examples to help investors navigate market trends effectively and capitalize on opportunities for passive income growth in the dynamic world of real estate investing. From understanding economic indicators to analyzing demographic shifts and regulatory changes, we cover all the essential elements necessary to maximize passive income growth and achieve long-term success in real estate. So, join us as we explore the art of navigating market trends and unlock the keys to financial freedom through passive income generation.

Chapter 11: Maverick Negotiation Tactics for Passive Real Estate Success

In the eleventh chapter of "Passive Income Powerhouse: Real Estate Riches on Autopilot," we dive into the realm of negotiation tactics specifically tailored for passive real estate success. This chapter is dedicated to equipping investors with the strategies and techniques necessary to secure favorable deals, maximize returns, and build wealth through real estate investments with minimal hands-on involvement.

Negotiation is a cornerstone of successful real estate investing, allowing investors to secure favorable terms, maximize profits, and mitigate risks. While negotiation tactics may vary depending on the specific circumstances of each transaction, certain maverick strategies can help passive investors stand out and achieve success in competitive markets.

One maverick negotiation tactic for passive real estate success is the power of patience. In a fast-paced market environment, it can be tempting to rush into a deal or succumb to pressure from sellers or agents. However, patient investors understand the importance of taking their time, conducting thorough due diligence, and waiting for the right opportunity to present itself. By remaining patient and disciplined, investors can avoid making hasty decisions and negotiate from a position of strength.

Moreover, maverick negotiators understand the importance of building rapport and establishing trust with sellers and agents. Rather than approaching negotiations as a zero-sum game, successful investors focus on building long-term relationships and finding mutually beneficial solutions. By demonstrating integrity, transparency, and professionalism, investors can foster trust and credibility, paving the way for smoother negotiations and better outcomes.

Another maverick negotiation tactic for passive real estate success is the art of creative problem-solving. In real estate transactions, issues and obstacles are inevitable, ranging from financing challenges to property defects or title issues. Successful negotiators approach these challenges with a solutions-oriented mindset, seeking creative alternatives and win-win solutions that address the interests of all parties involved. By thinking outside the box and leveraging their creativity, investors can overcome obstacles and turn challenges into opportunities for value creation.

Furthermore, maverick negotiators understand the importance of preparation and information asymmetry. Successful negotiations are often won or lost before the parties even sit down at the table. By conducting thorough research and due diligence, investors can arm themselves with valuable information and insights that give them a competitive advantage in negotiations. Whether it's knowing the seller's motivations, understanding market dynamics, or identifying potential deal-breakers, prepared investors are better equipped to negotiate effectively and achieve their objectives.

In this chapter, we provide practical guidance and real-world examples to help passive investors master the art of negotiation and achieve success in real estate investing. From the power of patience and building rapport to creative problem-solving and preparation, we cover all the essential elements necessary to negotiate like a maverick and unlock the keys to passive real estate success. So, join us as we explore the art of negotiation and empower investors to achieve their financial goals through passive income generation in the dynamic world of real estate.

Chapter 12: Tools for Passive Income Powerhouses

In the twelfth chapter of "Passive Income Powerhouse: Real Estate Riches on Autopilot," we explore the transformative role of technology and innovation in empowering passive income powerhouses to thrive in the dynamic world of real estate investing. This chapter is dedicated to unveiling the cutting-edge tools, platforms, and strategies that enable investors to streamline operations, optimize efficiency, and maximize returns with minimal manual effort.

Technology has revolutionized the way real estate investors conduct business, offering a wealth of tools and resources that facilitate every aspect of the investment process, from property sourcing and due diligence to management and analysis. By leveraging technology and innovation, passive income powerhouses can gain a competitive edge, scale their operations, and achieve greater success in their investment endeavors.

One of the most powerful technologies transforming real estate investing is data analytics and artificial intelligence (AI). These technologies enable investors to analyze vast amounts of data, identify trends and patterns, and make data-driven decisions with greater accuracy and precision. From predictive analytics that forecast market trends to machine learning algorithms that optimize property valuations, AI-powered tools empower investors to make smarter investment decisions and maximize returns.

Moreover, technology has revolutionized the way investors source and evaluate investment opportunities. Online platforms and marketplaces connect investors with a diverse range of properties, crowdfunding opportunities, and investment funds, allowing them to access deals from anywhere in the world. Virtual reality (VR) and augmented reality (AR) technologies further enhance the investment experience, enabling investors to tour properties remotely and visualize potential renovations or improvements before making a purchase.

Furthermore, technology has transformed property management, enabling investors to automate routine tasks, streamline communications, and optimize operational efficiency. Property management software and platforms automate rent collection, maintenance requests, and tenant communication, reducing administrative burdens and freeing up time for investors to focus on higher-value activities. Moreover, smart home technologies such as IoT devices and automated systems enhance property security, energy efficiency, and tenant satisfaction, ultimately driving higher returns and greater tenant retention.

In addition to streamlining operations, technology also facilitates better portfolio management and performance tracking. Real estate investment platforms and dashboards provide investors with real-time insights into their portfolio performance, cash flow projections, and return on investment (ROI), enabling them to monitor progress, identify areas for improvement, and make informed decisions to optimize portfolio returns.

In this chapter, we provide practical guidance and real-world examples to help passive income powerhouses harness the transformative power of technology and innovation in their real estate investment endeavors. From data analytics and AI to online platforms and smart home technologies, we cover all the essential tools and strategies necessary to achieve passive income success in the digital age. So, join us as we explore the cutting-edge technologies shaping the future of real estate investing and empower investors to unlock the full potential of passive income generation.

Chapter 13: Overcoming Passive Income Challenges

In the thirteenth chapter of "Passive Income Powerhouse: Real Estate Riches on Autopilot," we confront the inevitable challenges that passive income investors face and present strategies to navigate them effectively. This chapter is dedicated to equipping investors with the resilience, adaptability, and problem-solving skills necessary to overcome obstacles and achieve success in their real estate endeavors.

Passive income investing offers immense opportunities for wealth accumulation and financial freedom, but it's not without its challenges. From market volatility and regulatory changes to tenant issues and unexpected expenses, passive income investors must navigate a myriad of obstacles on their path to success. However, with the right mindset and strategies, these challenges can be turned into opportunities for growth and learning.

One of the most common challenges faced by passive income investors is market volatility. Real estate markets are subject to fluctuations in supply and demand, economic conditions, and investor sentiment, which can impact property values and rental income. To overcome this challenge, investors must adopt a long-term perspective and focus on building diversified portfolios that can withstand market fluctuations and deliver consistent returns over time.

Moreover, regulatory changes and legal issues can pose significant challenges for passive income investors. Changes in zoning laws, rent control regulations, or tax policies can impact property values, rental rates, and overall investment returns. To mitigate these risks, investors must stay informed about regulatory developments and seek expert advice when navigating legal issues or compliance requirements.

Tenant-related challenges, such as vacancies, non-payment of rent, or property damage, can also impact passive income streams and disrupt cash flow. To overcome these challenges, investors must implement effective tenant screening processes, maintain open lines of communication with tenants, and proactively address any issues that arise. Additionally, investors can leverage property management services or technology solutions to streamline tenant management and ensure a positive rental experience for all parties involved.

Furthermore, unexpected expenses such as maintenance repairs, property taxes, or insurance premiums can erode passive income and impact overall investment returns. To mitigate these risks, investors should budget for ongoing expenses, maintain adequate reserves, and conduct regular property inspections to identify potential issues before they escalate. Additionally, investors can explore cost-saving measures such as energy-efficient upgrades or preventative maintenance programs to reduce operating expenses and maximize cash flow.

In this chapter, we provide practical guidance and real-world examples to help passive income investors overcome common challenges and achieve success in their real estate endeavors. From navigating market volatility and regulatory changes to managing tenant issues and unexpected expenses, we cover all the essential strategies necessary to thrive in the dynamic world of passive income investing. So, join us as we explore the art of overcoming challenges and empower investors to achieve their financial goals through passive income generation in the real estate market.

Chapter 14: The Passive Income Powerhouse's Guide to Property Management

In the fourteenth chapter of "Passive Income Powerhouse: Real Estate Riches on Autopilot," we delve into the crucial aspects of property management that are essential for sustaining and growing a successful passive income portfolio. Effective property management is the backbone of any real estate investment strategy, ensuring that properties are well-maintained, tenants are satisfied, and income streams remain consistent. This chapter provides a comprehensive guide to mastering property management while maintaining a passive approach.

Effective property management involves overseeing the daily operations of rental properties, including tenant relations, maintenance, and financial management. For passive investors, the goal is to achieve these outcomes with minimal hands-on involvement, leveraging tools, technologies, and professional services to streamline processes and optimize efficiency.

One of the key elements of successful property management is tenant acquisition and retention. Finding and keeping reliable tenants is critical for maintaining steady rental income and minimizing vacancies. This starts with thorough tenant screening processes, which involve background checks, credit assessments, and verification of employment and rental history. By carefully selecting tenants who are likely to be responsible and financially stable, investors can reduce the risk of late payments, property damage, and evictions.

Tenant retention is equally important, as turnover can be costly and time-consuming. Creating a positive rental experience is crucial for retaining tenants. This can be achieved by maintaining open and effective communication, responding promptly to maintenance requests, and ensuring that the property is well-maintained and meets tenants' needs. Happy tenants are more likely to renew their leases, reducing vacancy rates and turnover costs.

Maintenance and repairs are another critical aspect of property management. Regular property inspections and preventative maintenance can help identify and address issues before they become major problems. This not only preserves the value of the property but also ensures tenant satisfaction. Investors can outsource maintenance tasks to professional property management companies or hire reliable contractors to handle repairs efficiently.

Financial management is also a cornerstone of effective property management. This involves keeping accurate records of income and expenses, budgeting for ongoing costs, and ensuring timely rent collection. Property management software can automate many of these tasks, providing real-time insights into financial performance and helping investors make informed decisions.

For passive investors, leveraging property management services can be a game-changer. Professional property management companies can handle all aspects of property management, from marketing and tenant screening to maintenance and financial reporting. While this involves an additional cost, it can save time and reduce the stress associated with managing rental properties, allowing investors to focus on expanding their portfolios and achieving their financial goals.

Technology plays a significant role in modern property management. Online platforms and apps facilitate tenant communication, rent collection, and maintenance requests, making the process more efficient and transparent. Smart home technologies can also enhance property management by improving security, energy efficiency, and overall tenant satisfaction.

In this chapter, we provide practical guidance and real-world examples to help passive investors master the art of property management. From tenant acquisition and retention to maintenance, financial management, and leveraging technology, we cover all the essential strategies necessary to ensure the smooth operation of rental properties and maximize passive income. Join us as we explore the passive income powerhouse's guide to property management and unlock the keys to sustained success in the real estate market.

Chapter 15: Scaling Your Passive Income Empire

In the fifteenth chapter of "Passive Income Powerhouse: Real Estate Riches on Autopilot," we delve into the strategies and approaches necessary for scaling your passive income empire. Building a successful real estate portfolio is just the beginning; to achieve long-term financial independence and maximize wealth, investors must focus on growth and expansion. This chapter provides a comprehensive guide to scaling your passive income empire effectively and sustainably.

Scaling a real estate investment portfolio involves increasing the number of properties owned, diversifying asset types and locations, and optimizing management processes to handle a larger portfolio efficiently. Successful expansion requires careful planning, strategic investment, and the ability to adapt to changing market conditions.

One of the foundational strategies for scaling your passive income empire is leveraging the power of financing. Utilizing various financing options such as traditional mortgages, refinancing, and private loans allows investors to acquire additional properties without depleting their capital reserves. Strategic use of leverage can significantly enhance portfolio growth and boost returns, but it also requires careful management to avoid overleveraging and financial risk.

Diversification is another critical strategy for scaling your passive income empire. By investing in different types of properties (e.g., residential, commercial, industrial) and across various geographic locations, investors can spread risk and reduce the impact of market fluctuations. Diversification also opens up new income streams and opportunities for growth, ensuring that the portfolio remains resilient in the face of economic changes.

Joint ventures and partnerships offer another pathway to expansion. By collaborating with other investors, real estate developers, or private equity firms, investors can pool resources, share expertise, and access larger or more complex deals than they could on their own. Partnerships can provide the capital, knowledge, and network necessary to scale rapidly and achieve significant growth.

Implementing robust property management systems and technologies is essential for managing a growing portfolio efficiently. As the number of properties increases, the complexity of managing them also rises. Property management software, automated rent collection systems, and maintenance management platforms can streamline operations, reduce administrative burdens, and ensure that properties are managed effectively. Outsourcing property management to professional firms can also free up time and resources, allowing investors to focus on strategic growth initiatives.

Reinvestment of profits is a powerful strategy for scaling a passive income empire. Rather than withdrawing rental income for personal use, reinvesting profits into acquiring new properties or upgrading existing ones can accelerate portfolio growth. Compound growth through reinvestment can exponentially increase the value and income potential of the portfolio over time.

Additionally, staying informed about market trends and emerging opportunities is crucial for successful expansion. Investors should continuously monitor economic indicators, demographic shifts, and regulatory changes to identify growth markets and high-potential investment opportunities. Adapting to market conditions and being proactive in seizing opportunities can drive sustained growth and long-term success.

In this chapter, we provide practical guidance and real-world examples to help investors scale their passive income empires. From leveraging financing and diversification to forming strategic partnerships, implementing advanced management systems, and reinvesting profits, we cover all the essential strategies necessary for effective and sustainable growth. Join us as we explore the art of scaling your passive income empire and unlock the keys to achieving financial independence and enduring prosperity in the real estate market.

Chapter 16: Your Journey to Real Estate Riches on Autopilot

In the final chapter of "Passive Income Powerhouse: Real Estate Riches on Autopilot," we bring together all the insights and strategies discussed throughout the book to help you map your unique path to real estate riches. This chapter serves as a comprehensive guide to planning, executing, and refining your passive income journey, ensuring that you achieve financial independence and long-term success with minimal active involvement.

Setting Clear Goals and Objectives

The first step in mapping your path to real estate riches is to set clear, measurable goals. Define what financial independence means to you, whether it's a specific monthly passive income target, a net worth milestone, or a particular lifestyle you aim to achieve. Your goals will guide your investment strategy and help you stay focused and motivated.

Developing a Strategic Plan

With your goals in mind, develop a strategic plan that outlines the steps necessary to achieve them. This plan should include:

- **Investment Criteria:** Define the types of properties you want to invest in, including location, property type, and expected return on investment (ROI).

- **Financing Strategy:** Determine how you will finance your investments, whether through traditional mortgages, private loans, partnerships, or a combination of these.

- **Acquisition Plan:** Outline how many properties you aim to acquire annually and the criteria for selecting them.

- **Management Plan:** Decide whether you will self-manage or hire a property management company, and establish systems for efficient property management.

Leveraging Technology and Automation

As discussed in earlier chapters, leveraging technology and automation is crucial for managing your real estate investments with minimal active involvement. Implement property management software, automated rent collection systems, and maintenance request platforms to streamline operations. Utilize data analytics and AI tools to make informed investment decisions and optimize portfolio performance.

Building a Diversified Portfolio

Diversification is key to mitigating risk and maximizing returns. Aim to build a portfolio that includes different types of properties (residential, commercial, industrial) across various geographic locations. This diversification will help protect your investments from market volatility and ensure a steady stream of passive income.

Continuously Educating Yourself

The real estate market is dynamic, and staying informed about trends, regulatory changes, and emerging opportunities is essential for long-term success. Continuously educate yourself by reading industry publications, attending seminars, and networking with other real estate professionals. Being proactive and knowledgeable will enable you to adapt to changes and seize new opportunities.

Monitoring and Adjusting Your Strategy

Regularly review your portfolio's performance and compare it against your goals. Use key performance indicators (KPIs) such as cash flow, ROI, occupancy rates, and maintenance costs to assess your progress. If you find that certain investments are underperforming, be prepared to adjust your strategy. This might involve selling underperforming properties, reinvesting profits into higher-yield opportunities, or adjusting your management approach.

Reinvesting Profits

Reinvesting profits is a powerful way to accelerate portfolio growth. Rather than withdrawing rental income for personal use, reinvest it into acquiring new properties or upgrading existing ones. This compounding effect can significantly enhance your portfolio's value and income potential over time.

Building a Support Network

Surround yourself with a network of professionals who can support your investment journey. This includes real estate agents, property managers, contractors, accountants, and legal advisors. A strong support network can provide valuable advice, streamline operations, and help you navigate challenges.

Celebrating Milestones and Successes

Finally, take the time to celebrate your milestones and successes along the way. Achieving financial independence through passive income is a significant accomplishment, and recognizing your progress will keep you motivated and focused on your long-term goals.

Your journey to real estate riches on autopilot is a continuous process of planning, execution, and refinement. By setting clear goals, leveraging technology, diversifying your portfolio, and staying informed, you can build a robust passive income stream that leads to financial independence and lasting wealth. This chapter provides a roadmap to guide you on your path, ensuring that you have the tools and strategies necessary to achieve success in the dynamic world of real estate investing.

Conclusion

As we reach the end of "Passive Income Powerhouse: Real Estate Riches on Autopilot," it's clear that the journey to achieving financial freedom through passive real estate investing is both an art and a science. This book has aimed to equip you with the knowledge, strategies, and tools necessary to build a thriving real estate portfolio that generates consistent and growing passive income with minimal active involvement.

Throughout the chapters, we've explored the foundational concepts of passive income in real estate, the potential of building your empire, and the importance of leveraging automation and technology. We've delved into identifying profitable properties, mastering the art of passive investing, and maximizing returns with minimal effort. Additionally, we discussed diversification strategies, tax optimization, navigating market trends, and employing maverick negotiation tactics.

We also emphasized the importance of effective property management and provided insights into overcoming the challenges that come with passive real estate investing. Finally, we mapped out the strategies for scaling your passive income empire and provided a comprehensive guide to planning and executing your journey towards real estate riches on autopilot.

The Road Ahead

The road to financial independence through real estate is not without its challenges, but with the right mindset, tools, and strategies, it's a journey that can lead to immense rewards. Here are some key takeaways to keep in mind as you continue on your path:

- **Continuous Learning:** The real estate market is dynamic and ever-changing. Stay informed about new trends, technologies, and strategies to remain competitive and optimize your portfolio.

- **Resilience and Adaptability:** Challenges and obstacles are inevitable. Approach them with a solutions-oriented mindset and be prepared to adapt your strategies as needed.

- **Leverage Technology:** Embrace technology and automation to streamline operations, enhance efficiency, and reduce the need for hands-on management.

- **Build a Strong Network:** Surround yourself with a team of professionals who can provide valuable support, advice, and services to help you achieve your goals.

- **Stay Focused on Your Goals:** Regularly review your progress and adjust your strategies to stay aligned with your long-term financial objectives.

Your Path to Financial Freedom

Achieving financial freedom through passive real estate investing is a journey that requires dedication, strategic planning, and a proactive approach. By applying the principles and strategies outlined in this book, you can build a robust and diversified real estate portfolio that generates steady passive income and paves the way to lasting wealth.

Remember, the key to success lies in taking consistent, informed action and continuously refining your approach. The road to real estate riches is a marathon, not a sprint. Stay committed to your goals, leverage the resources available to you, and keep pushing forward.

Final Thoughts

Thank you for embarking on this journey with "Passive Income Powerhouse: Real Estate Riches on Autopilot." We hope this book has provided you with the insights, inspiration, and practical guidance needed to achieve your financial goals through passive real estate investing.

Here's to your success and the prosperous journey ahead as you build your passive income powerhouse and achieve the financial freedom you desire.

www.ingramcontent.com/pod-product-compliance
Lightning Source LLC
Chambersburg PA
CBHW071952210526
45479CB00003B/910